# On Route

## Great Yarmouth

Long narrow town hemmed in between the sea and the River Yare, Great Yarmouth's economy was based almost entirely upon its herring fisheries until the mid 18th century. With the arrival of the early holidaymaker the town began to turn away from its base upon the riverside quays to its long sandy sea front, but today there is a happy balance between the still busy quays overlooked by fine 18th century buildings (South Quay), the mid-Victorian sea front embellished with every conceivable 20th century pleasure facility, and the narrow 'Rows', medieval alleys running eastwards from South Quay. These rows were badly damaged in the 1939–1945 war, but those that remain still contain many interesting features.

Great Yarmouth is too extensive to describe adequately, but see especially the Elizabethan House (containing a museum) and the Old Merchant's House, both on South Quay, the medieval town
*Continued on page 21.*

1. *On Yarmouth Quay*

## Burgh Castle

Drive beyond the unexceptional village and park near the church, an over-restored building with a round Norman tower topped with brick. Follow signs for about half a mile to the impressive remains of GARIANNONUM, a Roman fort built towards the end of the third century. Constructed of flint and brick, the walls of the fort remain as high as 15 feet and there are round bastion towers at intervals. It is also possible to drive down to Burgh Castle Marina and the hospitable Fisherman's Bar (see Route Directions opposite).

2. *Burgh Castle*

## Fritton Church

This is a thatched building with a round tower. . . the second of many which we shall see on our Broadland journey. The interior contains a beautiful little apsidal (semi-circular) Norman chancel, whose entrance arch is decorated with medieval paintings, a 15th century painting of St. Christopher on the north wall, and a Jacobean three-decker pulpit.

## Fritton Lake

Part of the Somerleyton Estate (see page 5), Fritton Lake was known as Fritton Decoy, as it used to be equipped for the taking of wildfowl. There are now beautiful waterside gardens, with opportunities for boating and fishing on this attractive two mile long, tree bordered lake. There is a tea-room, and possibilities for picnicking.

3. *Fritton Lake*

## St. Olave's Priory

The ruins of a 13th century Augustinian Priory, a little way down a small track marked 'Priory Farm'. Not very dramatic, but the remains include a 14th century undercroft, the arches of which are an early example of the use of brick.

## St. Olave's Bridge

Marks a popular mooring place on the River Waveney, with the mellow brick and partly timbered Bell Inn not far away.

4. *St. Olave's Bridge*

3

# Map 2

| Miles | | kms Ref. Miles | Directions | Sign-posted |
|---|---|---|---|---|

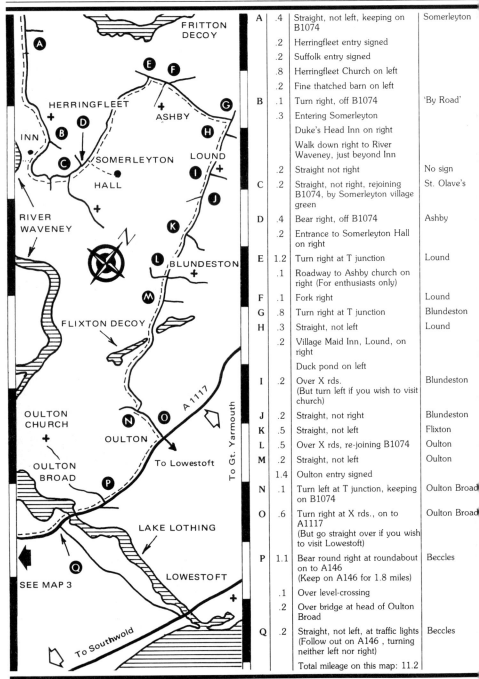

| Ref. | Miles | Directions | Sign-posted |
|---|---|---|---|
| A | .4 | Straight, not left, keeping on B1074 | Somerleyton |
|  | .2 | Herringfleet entry signed |  |
|  | .2 | Suffolk entry signed |  |
|  | .8 | Herringfleet Church on left |  |
|  | .2 | Fine thatched barn on left |  |
| B | .1 | Turn right, off B1074 | 'By Road' |
|  | .3 | Entering Somerleyton |  |
|  |  | Duke's Head Inn on right |  |
|  |  | Walk down right to River Waveney, just beyond Inn |  |
|  | .2 | Straight not right | No sign |
| C | .2 | Straight, not right, rejoining B1074, by Somerleyton village green | St. Olave's |
| D | .4 | Bear right, off B1074 | Ashby |
|  | .2 | Entrance to Somerleyton Hall on right |  |
| E | 1.2 | Turn right at T junction | Lound |
|  | .1 | Roadway to Ashby church on right (For enthusiasts only) |  |
| F | .1 | Fork right | Lound |
| G | .8 | Turn right at T junction | Blundeston |
| H | .3 | Straight, not left | Lound |
|  | .2 | Village Maid Inn, Lound, on right |  |
|  |  | Duck pond on left |  |
| I | .2 | Over X rds. (But turn left if you wish to visit church) | Blundeston |
| J | .2 | Straight, not right | Blundeston |
| K | .5 | Straight, not left | Flixton |
| L | .5 | Over X rds, re-joining B1074 | Oulton |
| M | .2 | Straight, not left | Oulton |
|  | 1.4 | Oulton entry signed |  |
| N | .1 | Turn left at T junction, keeping on B1074 | Oulton Broad |
| O | .6 | Turn right at X rds., on to A1117 (But go straight over if you wish to visit Lowestoft) | Oulton Broad |
| P | 1.1 | Bear round right at roundabout on to A146 (Keep on A146 for 1.8 miles) | Beccles |
|  | .1 | Over level-crossing |  |
|  | .2 | Over bridge at head of Oulton Broad |  |
| Q | .2 | Straight, not left, at traffic lights (Follow out on A146, turning neither left nor right) | Beccles |
|  |  | Total mileage on this map: 11.2 |  |

4

# BROADLAND COUNTRY BY CAR

Including Yarmouth, Burgh Castle, Fritton, Somerleyton, Lowestoft, Oulton, Beccles, Norwich, Coltishall, Wroxham, Hickling, Horsey, Caister Castle, Irstead, Horning, Ludham, Womack Staithe, Potter Heigham, Ranworth, Salhouse.

This guide book contains exact but simple directions for the motorist who wishes to combine visits to such well known centres as Norwich, Caister, Great Yarmouth, Lowestoft, Wroxham and Horning, with an exploration of the quiet lanes leading to Broadland's hidden waterside places, many of which are not at all easy to find without detailed guidance.

The 'Main Circle' Route (Maps 1 – 10) shown on the Key Map opposite covers 118 miles, and mainly follows around the outer confines of Broadland. If from time to time we have had to lead you away from the water we would excuse ourselves by claiming that there sometimes appears to be no satisfactory alternative.

The 'Main Circle' Route is too long for a leisurely day's journey and you will note from the Key Map that we have included certain cross routes to break this up into smaller circles. However if your time is limited, may we recommend the 'Broadland Special', with a start from Wroxham on Map 11, then Map 2 as far as Burgh St. Margaret, A1064 to Acle, and return to Wroxham on the end of Map 14 and the whole of Map 15.

It should be stressed that each route being circular, may be started and finished at any point suitable to you.

# HOW TO USE YOUR BOOK ON THE ROUTE

Each double page makes up a complete picture of the country ahead of you. On the left you will find a one inch to the mile strip map, with the route marked by a series of dashes. Direction is always from top to bottom, so that the map may be looked at in conjunction with the 'directions to the driver', with which it is cross referenced by a letter itemising each junction point. This enables the driver to have exact guidance every time an opportunity for changing direction occurs, even if it is only 'Keep straight, not left!'

With mileage intervals shown, the driver should even have warning when to expect these 'moments of decision', and if a signpost exists we have used this to help you, with the 'Signposted . . .' column. However re-signing is always in progress, and this may lead to slight differences in sign marking in some cases . . . So beware of freshly erected signs.

We have also included a description of the towns and villages through which you will pass, together with some photographs to illustrate the route.

There is no doubt that some Broadland enthusiasts will be horrified at the idea of 'Broadland by car', but if you use your car with care, this guide will at least bring you to the threshold of many enchanting waterside places. When you arrive at these 'thresholds' do be prepared to leave your car and walk (or perhaps hire a small boat, when the opportunity occurs), for little will be gained if you merely set out to drive mile after mile without pausing for reflection, or seeking quiet places away from the roads. But whatever your objective, may we conclude by wishing you 'good hunting' in your exploration of this secret, watery landscape, with its wide skies, its fabulous churches, its fascinating wildlife, and its friendly and relaxed inhabitants.

Compiled by PETER and HELEN TITCHMARSH
Photography by ALAN and PETER TITCHMARSH

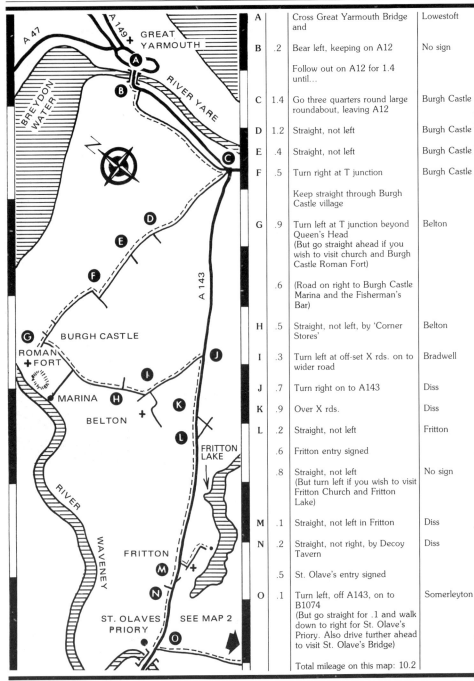

| | Ref. | Miles | Directions | Sign-posted |
|---|---|---|---|---|
| A | | | Cross Great Yarmouth Bridge and | Lowestoft |
| B | | .2 | Bear left, keeping on A12 | No sign |
| | | | Follow out on A12 for 1.4 until... | |
| C | | 1.4 | Go three quarters round large roundabout, leaving A12 | Burgh Castle |
| D | | 1.2 | Straight, not left | Burgh Castle |
| E | | .4 | Straight, not left | Burgh Castle |
| F | | .5 | Turn right at T junction | Burgh Castle |
| | | | Keep straight through Burgh Castle village | |
| G | | .9 | Turn left at T junction beyond Queen's Head (But go straight ahead if you wish to visit church and Burgh Castle Roman Fort) | Belton |
| | | .6 | (Road on right to Burgh Castle Marina and the Fisherman's Bar) | |
| H | | .5 | Straight, not left, by 'Corner Stores' | Belton |
| I | | .3 | Turn left at off-set X rds. on to wider road | Bradwell |
| J | | .7 | Turn right on to A143 | Diss |
| K | | .9 | Over X rds. | Diss |
| L | | .2 | Straight, not left | Fritton |
| | | .6 | Fritton entry signed | |
| | | .8 | Straight, not left (But turn left if you wish to visit Fritton Church and Fritton Lake) | No sign |
| M | | .1 | Straight, not left in Fritton | Diss |
| N | | .2 | Straight, not right, by Decoy Tavern | Diss |
| | | .5 | St. Olave's entry signed | |
| O | | .1 | Turn left, off A143, on to B1074 (But go straight for .1 and walk down to right for St. Olave's Priory. Also drive further ahead to visit St. Olave's Bridge) | Somerleyton |
| | | | Total mileage on this map: 10.2 | |

# On Route

### Herringfleet Church
Is situated nearly two miles away from the present village. It has a very early Norman round tower (see the 'Saxon style' triangular headed windows), a hatched roof and a pretty little Norman south doorway. We liked the quaint, dusty early 19th century flavour of the interior . . . so much in contrast with the bright and immaculately restored church at Fritton (see page 3).

### Somerleyton
A Victorian estate village with cottages and school attractively grouped around a wide green, all the work of self-made squire, Sir Samuel Peto, railway magnate and builder of Lowestoft harbour. It is possible to walk down by the Duke's Head (see Route Directions) to the banks of the Waveney.

### Somerleyton Hall
An early Victorian mansion built around a Tudor-Jacobean shell by Sir Samuel Peto (see Somerleyton, above) to the designs of John Thomas, a protégé of Barry. See the splendidly opulent interior, the beautiful gardens with their extensive maze of clipped yews concealing a pagoda centrepiece. Other attractions include a nature trail, a miniature railway, children's farm and tea-room.

### Ashby Church
Isolated building lying up a farm road half a mile off our route (see Route Directions). It has Norman origins, but does not in our view justify the diversion.

### Lound
We liked the duck pond and the little Village Maid Inn close by, but there appears to be little else of interest apart from the church. This has a round tower, but its exterior is otherwise rather severe. However the interior has been most attractively restored and refurnished by that 20th century genius, Sir Ninian Comper. See especially the gilded font cover.

### Lowestoft
Is really outside the confines of this guide, but a diversion to this busy holiday resort and fishing port is well worthwhile. Fishing and boating activity centres on the new twin bascule lifting bridge over the entrance to Lake Lothing, while holiday activities lie behind the sands to the south of the bridge. Do not miss St. Margaret's church on the road in from Oulton . . . a fine 15th century building. Collectors of 'ultimates' will be interested to learn that the Ness marks England's most easterly point.

### Oulton Church
Tucked away well beyond bustling Oulton, the partly Norman church looks out westwards over the marshes to the River Waveney. This cruciform building has a stout brick tower, and inside there is a pleasant 15th century font with lions and angels. George Borrow had a house near here beside the Broad, but it has long since been swept away.

### Oulton Broad (See Page 7)

*1. Herringfleet Church*

*2. River Waveney, Somerleyton*

*3. Somerleyton Hall*    Photograph by Claridge & Griffee

*4. Oulton Broad*

5

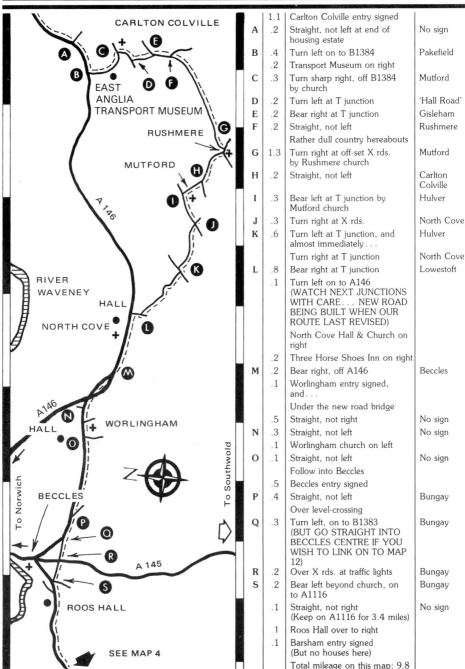

| Ref. | Miles | Directions | Sign-posted |
|---|---|---|---|
| | 1.1 | Carlton Colville entry signed | |
| A | .2 | Straight, not left at end of housing estate | No sign |
| B | .4 | Turn left on to B1384 | Pakefield |
| | .2 | Transport Museum on right | |
| C | .3 | Turn sharp right, off B1384 by church | Mutford |
| D | .2 | Turn left at T junction | 'Hall Road' |
| E | .2 | Bear right at T junction | Gisleham |
| F | .2 | Straight, not left | Rushmere |
| | | Rather dull country hereabouts | |
| G | 1.3 | Turn right at off-set X rds. by Rushmere church | Mutford |
| H | .2 | Straight, not left | Carlton Colville |
| I | .3 | Bear left at T junction by Mutford church | Hulver |
| J | .3 | Turn right at X rds. | North Cove |
| K | .6 | Turn left at T junction, and almost immediately... | Hulver |
| | | Turn right at T junction | North Cove |
| L | .8 | Bear right at T junction | Lowestoft |
| | .1 | Turn left on to A146 (WATCH NEXT JUNCTIONS WITH CARE... NEW ROAD BEING BUILT WHEN OUR ROUTE LAST REVISED) | |
| | | North Cove Hall & Church on right | |
| | .2 | Three Horse Shoes Inn on right | |
| M | .2 | Bear right, off A146 | Beccles |
| | .1 | Worlingham entry signed, and... | |
| | | Under the new road bridge | |
| | .5 | Straight, not right | No sign |
| N | .3 | Straight, not left | No sign |
| | .1 | Worlingham church on left | |
| O | .1 | Straight, not left | No sign |
| | | Follow into Beccles | |
| | .5 | Beccles entry signed | |
| P | .4 | Straight, not left | Bungay |
| | | Over level-crossing | |
| Q | .3 | Turn left, on to B1383 (BUT GO STRAIGHT INTO BECCLES CENTRE IF YOU WISH TO LINK ON TO MAP 12) | Bungay |
| R | .2 | Over X rds. at traffic lights | Bungay |
| S | .2 | Bear left beyond church, on to A1116 | Bungay |
| | .1 | Straight, not right (Keep on A1116 for 3.4 miles) | No sign |
| | .1 | Roos Hall over to right | |
| | .1 | Barsham entry signed (But no houses here) | |
| | | Total mileage on this map: 9.8 | |

# On Route

## Oulton Broad (See page 4)

Our road crosses the lock connecting the eastern end of Oulton Broad with Lake Lothing and the sea, and at the western end of Oulton Broad there is a dyke linking it to the River Waveney and the Broadland water system . . . so here indeed 'Broadland meets the sea'. It is a bright, busy spot with many boatyards, and an attractive public park, all overlooked by old malt houses on the quay, and the large Victorian Wherry Hotel beside our bridge. We stopped here one Saturday lunchtime and were fascinated by the stout efforts of 'first-timers' taking out their hired craft at the beginning of a week's cruise.

## Carlton Colville

A large parish lying to the south of Oulton Broad. Try to visit the East Anglia Transport Museum in Chapel Street, which has an interesting collection of vehicles from the past, and a tram service at weekends.

## Rushmere

Scattered parish with only its church and attractive early 19th century rectory lying upon our route. The church is thatched and has yet another round tower. However when we called it was closed due to its roof being in a dangerous state and we wondered if it will ever be repaired.

## Mutford Church

This is a round towered building standing by itself on a little knoll away from a rather scrappy village. However, having once located the key in the village, we were attracted by the pleasantly simple flavour of the interior with its early 19th century pews, its fragment of medieval wall painting, and its mellow brick floors. Do not miss the relatively unusual 14th century 'Galilee' porch.

## North Cove

North Cove Hall, a handsome mellow brick Georgian building, stands in a small park close by the road. The church is not far beyond, with the attractive Three Horseshoes Inn beside it. The church is a long thatched building with a slender tower faced with brick. There is a small Norman south doorway, and inside, a most interesting series of 14th century wall paintings illustrating the Crucifixion and the Last Day of Judgement.

## Worlingham

The church was largely re-built by the Victorians, but it does contain one of Sir Francis Chantrey's earliest monuments . . . that to Robert Sparrow, builder of the lovely Worlingham Hall (sometimes open by prior appointment).

## Beccles (See page 25)

## Roos Hall

Impressive 16th century mellow brick manor house with a tall step gable, lying quietly beyond a meadow just outside Beccles.

*1. Mutford Church*

*2. Beccles Church*

*3. Beccles Bridge*

7

# Map 4

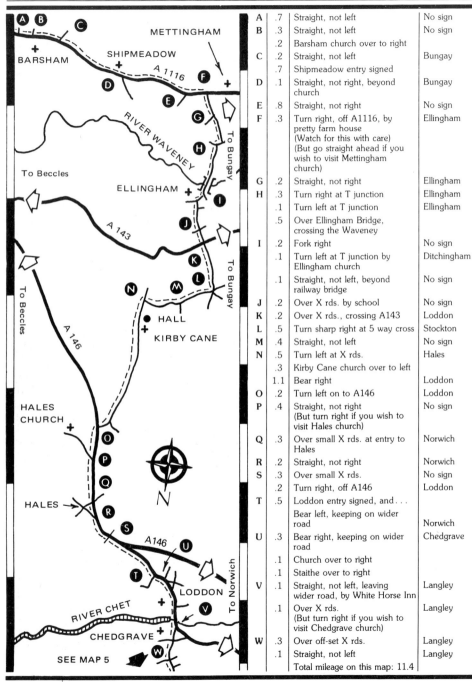

| Ref | Miles | Directions | Signposted |
|---|---|---|---|
| A | .7 | Straight, not left | No sign |
| B | .3 | Straight, not left | No sign |
|  | .2 | Barsham church over to right |  |
| C | .2 | Straight, not left | Bungay |
|  | .7 | Shipmeadow entry signed |  |
| D | .1 | Straight, not right, beyond church | Bungay |
| E | .8 | Straight, not right | No sign |
| F | .3 | Turn right, off A1116, by pretty farm house (Watch for this with care) (But go straight ahead if you wish to visit Mettingham church) | Ellingham |
| G | .2 | Straight, not right | Ellingham |
| H | .3 | Turn right at T junction | Ellingham |
|  | .1 | Turn left at T junction | Ellingham |
|  | .5 | Over Ellingham Bridge, crossing the Waveney |  |
| I | .2 | Fork right | No sign |
|  | .1 | Turn left at T junction by Ellingham church | Ditchingham |
|  | .1 | Straight, not left, beyond railway bridge | No sign |
| J | .2 | Over X rds. by school | No sign |
| K | .2 | Over X rds., crossing A143 | Loddon |
| L | .5 | Turn sharp right at 5 way cross | Stockton |
| M | .4 | Straight, not left | No sign |
| N | .5 | Turn left at X rds. | Hales |
|  | .3 | Kirby Cane church over to left |  |
|  | 1.1 | Bear right | Loddon |
| O | .2 | Turn left on to A146 | Loddon |
| P | .4 | Straight, not right (But turn right if you wish to visit Hales church) | No sign |
| Q | .3 | Over small X rds. at entry to Hales | Norwich |
| R | .2 | Straight, not right | Norwich |
| S | .3 | Over small X rds. | No sign |
|  | .2 | Turn right, off A146 | Loddon |
| T | .5 | Loddon entry signed, and . . . |  |
|  |  | Bear left, keeping on wider road | Norwich |
| U | .3 | Bear right, keeping on wider road | Chedgrave |
|  | .1 | Church over to right |  |
|  | .1 | Staithe over to right |  |
| V | .1 | Straight, not left, leaving wider road, by White Horse Inn | Langley |
|  | .1 | Over X rds. (But turn right if you wish to visit Chedgrave church) | Langley |
| W | .3 | Over off-set X rds. | Langley |
|  | .1 | Straight, not left | Langley |
|  |  | Total mileage on this map: 11.4 |  |

# On Route

1. Barsham Rectory

### Barsham

Church and rectory lie by themselves in a quiet park-like setting away from the road. The church has a round tower with a minute spire and has an interior full of atmosphere. Nelson's mother, Catherine Suckling was born in the nearby 17th century rectory which has gorgeously curving Dutch gables.

### Mettingham Castle

(Go straight ahead at Point F, turn left beyond church, and then left again.)

This was built in about 1345 by Sir John de Norwich, 'Admiral of the Northern Fleet', and one of England's first great sea captains. The gatehouse is the only part of the original building still standing, but it is a gauntly impressive structure. (Not open to the public, but it is visible from the road.)

### Mettingham Church

Has a round tower, a well ornamented Norman north doorway, and an attractive font with lions and angels around its top, and lions at its base.

### Ellingham

A delightful riverside spot, complete with white weather-boarded mill, a little Gothick miller's house, and a square towered church a short distance beyond. Here are some box pews and a 16th century wall monument, but little else of interest.

2. Mettingham Gatehouse   3. Hales Church

### Kirby Cane

The church has an Anglo-Saxon round tower and an interesting Norman south doorway. Inside there is a 14th century octagonal font, a pleasantly plain tomb chest (1593) and an early Jacobean pulpit. From the churchyard one can obtain glimpses of the mellow brick Hall, but its handsome Georgian front unfortunately faces away from us.

### Hales Church

Stands sad and empty, about a mile from the village. However its apsidal chancel, and Norman north and south doors, its round tower and thatched roof, together provide a fair indication of how a Norfolk church must have looked in Norman times.

### Loddon

Bright little market town with many attractive 17th and 18th century houses, shops and inns. The impressive church lies beyond the rough 'square', and although over-restored, contains many features of interest. See especially the painting of Sir James Hobart and his wife, the tomb chest to James Hobart and his wife, with brasses, and the effigy in white marble of Lady Williamson.

4. Lady Williamson, Loddon

Loddon Staithe is overlooked by yet another white weather-boarded mill, and is a most attractively laid out 'marina' development complete with car park and boat yards. This is the navigable head of the River Chet, which runs into the Yare about three miles away.

### Chedgrave

Now almost part of Loddon, it has a small Norman church on high ground to its east, from where there are views out over the River Chet.

4. Loddon Staithe

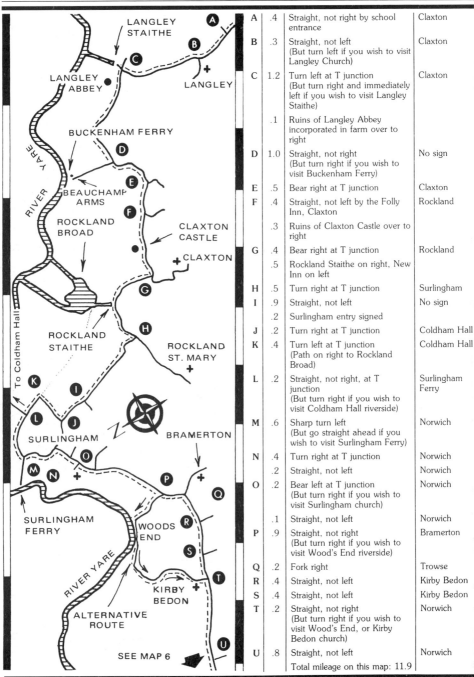

| | kms Ref. Miles | Directions | Sign-posted |
|---|---|---|---|
| A | .4 | Straight, not right by school entrance | Claxton |
| B | .3 | Straight, not left (But turn left if you wish to visit Langley Church) | Claxton |
| C | 1.2 | Turn left at T junction (But turn right and immediately left if you wish to visit Langley Staithe) | Claxton |
| | .1 | Ruins of Langley Abbey incorporated in farm over to right | |
| D | 1.0 | Straight, not right (But turn right if you wish to visit Buckenham Ferry) | No sign |
| E | .5 | Bear right at T junction | Claxton |
| F | .4 | Straight, not left by the Folly Inn, Claxton | Rockland |
| | .3 | Ruins of Claxton Castle over to right | |
| G | .4 | Bear right at T junction | Rockland |
| | .5 | Rockland Staithe on right, New Inn on left | |
| H | .5 | Turn right at T junction | Surlingham |
| I | .9 | Straight, not left | No sign |
| | .2 | Surlingham entry signed | |
| J | .2 | Turn right at T junction | Coldham Hall |
| K | .4 | Turn left at T junction (Path on right to Rockland Broad) | Coldham Hall |
| L | .2 | Straight, not right, at T junction (But turn right if you wish to visit Coldham Hall riverside) | Surlingham Ferry |
| M | .6 | Sharp turn left (But go straight ahead if you wish to visit Surlingham Ferry) | Norwich |
| N | .4 | Turn right at T junction | Norwich |
| | .2 | Straight, not left | Norwich |
| O | .2 | Bear left at T junction (But turn right if you wish to visit Surlingham church) | Norwich |
| | .1 | Straight, not left | Norwich |
| P | .9 | Straight, not right (But turn right if you wish to visit Wood's End riverside) | Bramerton |
| Q | .2 | Fork right | Trowse |
| R | .4 | Straight, not left | Kirby Bedon |
| S | .4 | Straight, not left | Kirby Bedon |
| T | .2 | Straight, not right (But turn right if you wish to visit Wood's End, or Kirby Bedon church) | Norwich |
| U | .8 | Straight, not left | Norwich |
| | | Total mileage on this map: 11.9 | |

# On Route

### Langley
Langley Park, a handsome 18th century mansion inspired by William Kent's designs for Holkham Hall, is now a school and is not open to the public. The church is pleasantly sited on the edge of the park. The interior of this 13th and 14th century building has a late 18th century flavour, with box pews and three-decker pulpit.

### Langley Staithe
This small dyke branching off the Yare lies just off our route beyond the little Wherry Inn, and is a quiet place at the end of a short rough track.

### Langley Abbey
The remains of a Premonstratensian Abbey (founded 1195) are incorporated into a farm to our right. (Not open to the public.)

### Buckenham 'Ferry'
There is no longer any ferry here, but there is a good road down to the Beauchamp Arms, which is in a pleasant setting beside the Yare.

### Claxton Castle
The ruins of a 15th century castle are visible from the road, in the grounds of Claxton Manor Farm. (Not open to the public.)

### Claxton Church
Pleasant little church on high ground above the marshy Yare valley, with a brick south porch, a font with lions and heraldry, box pews, and an attractive wall monument (to Henry Gawdy).

### Rockland Staithe
Delightful grass bordered staithe beside the road, overlooked by the hospitable New Inn. There is good fishing on Rockland Broad (about a quarter of a mile down the dyke).

### Coldham Hall
Attractive mellow brick and thatch inn looking out over a wide grassy quay bordering the Yare, complete with boatyard and sailing club.

### Surlingham Ferry (No ferry for vehicles)
The Ferry House is a pleasant white painted inn, and from its large car park beside the River Yare, one can look upstream to Surlingham church.

### Surlingham Church
There are pleasant views of river and marshes from the churchyard here. The beautiful little interior contains an octagonal font with lions and angels, and a most attractive modern lectern of carved wood. Do not miss the little owl at the base.

### Bramerton Woods End
One of the loveliest Yare riverside places, with woods overlooking the water, wide grassy banks, and a hospitable hotel at a wide bend in the river.
*(Note: It is possible at present to drive down here from Point P. Keep along the riverside, past the Woods End Hotel, and re-join the main route at Point T.)*

### Kirby Bedon (See Page 13)

1. At Buckenham Ferry          2. At Coldham Hall

3. Rockland Staithe

4. At Surlingham Ferry

5. Bramerton Woods End

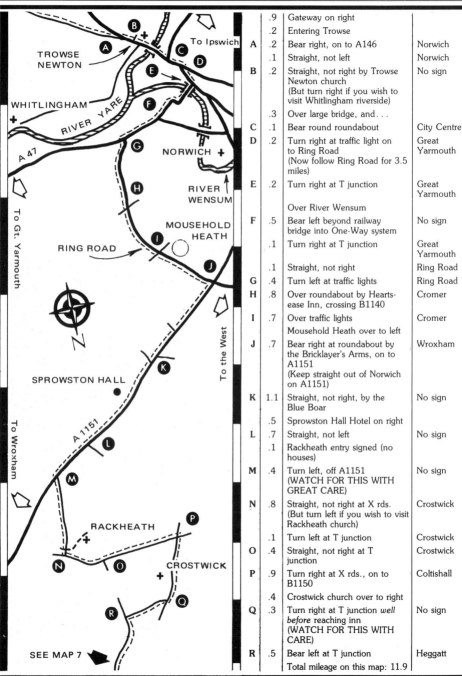

| | | | | |
|---|---|---|---|---|
| | | .9 | Gateway on right | |
| | | .2 | Entering Trowse | |
| | A | .2 | Bear right, on to A146 | Norwich |
| | | .1 | Straight, not left | Norwich |
| | B | .2 | Straight, not right by Trowse Newton church (But turn right if you wish to visit Whitlingham riverside) | No sign |
| | | .3 | Over large bridge, and. . . | |
| | C | .1 | Bear round roundabout | City Centre |
| | D | .2 | Turn right at traffic light on to Ring Road (Now follow Ring Road for 3.5 miles) | Great Yarmouth |
| | E | .2 | Turn right at T junction | Great Yarmouth |
| | | | Over River Wensum | |
| | F | .5 | Bear left beyond railway bridge into One-Way system | No sign |
| | | .1 | Turn right at T junction | Great Yarmouth |
| | | .1 | Straight, not right | Ring Road |
| | G | .4 | Turn left at traffic lights | Ring Road |
| | H | .8 | Over roundabout by Hearts-ease Inn, crossing B1140 | Cromer |
| | I | .7 | Over traffic lights | Cromer |
| | | | Mousehold Heath over to left | |
| | J | .7 | Bear right at roundabout by the Bricklayer's Arms, on to A1151 (Keep straight out of Norwich on A1151) | Wroxham |
| | K | 1.1 | Straight, not right, by the Blue Boar | No sign |
| | | .5 | Sprowston Hall Hotel on right | |
| | L | .7 | Straight, not left | No sign |
| | | .1 | Rackheath entry signed (no houses) | |
| | M | .4 | Turn left, off A1151 (WATCH FOR THIS WITH GREAT CARE) | No sign |
| | N | .8 | Straight, not right at X rds. (But turn left if you wish to visit Rackheath church) | Crostwick |
| | | .1 | Turn left at T junction | Crostwick |
| | O | .4 | Straight, not right at T junction | Crostwick |
| | P | .9 | Turn right at X rds., on to B1150 | Coltishall |
| | | .4 | Crostwick church over to right | |
| | Q | .3 | Turn right at T junction *well before* reaching inn (WATCH FOR THIS WITH CARE) | No sign |
| | R | .5 | Bear left at T junction | Heggatt |
| | | | Total mileage on this map: 11.9 | |

# On Route

**Kirby Bedon** (See Page 10)

Has a re-built church standing close to its handsome Georgian rectory, both of which are opposite the stark round tower of a second (ruined) church.

**Trowse Newton**

Although this lies across the river from Norwich it is all but overwhelmed by it. However if you can brave the traffic, stop to look at the church here, for the sake of the fine east window tracery, the vaulted porch and the figures grouped around the pulpit. (David with harp, plus two trumpet-blowing angels.)

**Whitlingham Riverside**

This diversion of nearly two miles takes us along a pleasant open road, much of it very close to the banks of the Yare. There are excellent picnic possibilities, but beware of crowds at peak times. The ruins of the church in the woods to our right near the end of the road are not worth visiting.

**Norwich**

Is really too important to be dealt with here, but those on a brief diversion from our route should perhaps concentrate on the Cathedral, with its 316 foot high spire (second only to Salisbury), the great Norman Castle, with its collection of paintings, historical relics and natural history items, the colourful Market Place, the City Hall, opened by George VI in 1938, the Guildhall, the Church of St. Peter Mancroft, the 17th century Assembly House, and the beautifully preserved 16th century street, Elm Hill. It is indeed 'a fine city' and obviously merits a far more detailed description than we can provide here.

**Mousehold Heath**

Extensive common land, to the left of our route beyond Point I, from whence there are fine views out over the city of Norwich. Mousehold Heath was immortalised by 'Old' John Crome, who with John Cotman, were the most important members of the 'Norwich School' of artists.

**Rackheath Church**

Stands by itself in quiet fields, in an overgrown churchyard lined with beech trees, and it is hard to appreciate that it stands no more than five miles from the very centre of bustling Norwich. If you can gain entry to this normally locked church, do not miss the octagonal 17th century font with its angels heads and coats of arms.

**Crostwick Church**

Lies away from the road, beyond a small bracken covered common, with its pleasant Perpendicular tower visible amongst the trees. However its interior is rather sad, with poor 19th century woodwork, a fragment of medieval wall painting, and two solitary old benches at the rear.

**Horstead Mill** (See Page 14)

This is a sad spot, for until it was destroyed by fire in 1963, there stood here a really beautiful weather-boarded mill. Now it has gone, but the weir still marks the head of navigation on the River Bure.

*1. Riverside at Whitlingham*

*2. Pull's Ferry, Norwich*   Photograph by Jarrold & Sons Ltd.

*3. Prince's Street, Norwich*     *4. City Hall, Norwich*
Photographs by Jarrold & Sons Ltd.

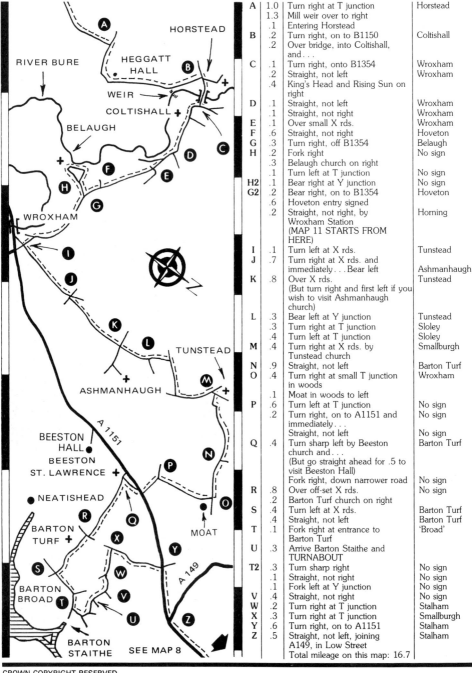

| | kms/Miles | Directions | Signposted |
|---|---|---|---|
| A | 1.0 | Turn right at T junction | Horstead |
| | 1.3 | Mill weir over to right | |
| | .1 | Entering Horstead | |
| B | .2 | Turn right, on to B1150 | Coltishall |
| | .2 | Over bridge, into Coltishall, and... | |
| C | .1 | Turn right, onto B1354 | Wroxham |
| | .2 | Straight, not left | Wroxham |
| | .4 | King's Head and Rising Sun on right | |
| D | .1 | Straight, not left | Wroxham |
| | .1 | Straight, not right | Wroxham |
| E | .1 | Over small X rds. | Wroxham |
| F | .6 | Straight, not right | Hoveton |
| G | .3 | Turn right, off B1354 | Belaugh |
| H | .2 | Fork right | No sign |
| | .3 | Belaugh church on right | |
| | .1 | Turn left at T junction | No sign |
| H2 | .1 | Bear right at Y junction | No sign |
| G2 | .2 | Bear right, on to B1354 | Hoveton |
| | .6 | Hoveton entry signed | |
| | .2 | Straight, not right, by Wroxham Station (MAP 11 STARTS FROM HERE) | Horning |
| I | .1 | Turn left at X rds. | Tunstead |
| J | .7 | Turn right at X rds. and immediately...Bear left | Ashmanhaugh |
| K | .8 | Over X rds. (But turn right and first left if you wish to visit Ashmanhaugh church) | Tunstead |
| L | .3 | Bear left at Y junction | Tunstead |
| | .3 | Turn right at T junction | Sloley |
| | .4 | Turn left at T junction | Sloley |
| M | .4 | Turn right at X rds. by Tunstead church | Smallburgh |
| N | .9 | Straight, not left | Barton Turf |
| O | .4 | Turn right at small T junction in woods | Wroxham |
| | .1 | Moat in woods to left | |
| P | .6 | Turn left at T junction | No sign |
| | .2 | Turn right, on to A1151 and immediately... | No sign |
| | | Straight, not left | No sign |
| Q | .4 | Turn sharp left by Beeston church and... (But go straight ahead for .5 to visit Beeston Hall) | Barton Turf |
| | | Fork right, down narrower road | No sign |
| R | .8 | Over off-set X rds. | No sign |
| | .2 | Barton Turf church on right | |
| S | .4 | Turn left at X rds. | Barton Turf |
| | .4 | Straight, not left | Barton Turf |
| T | .1 | Fork right at entrance to Barton Turf | 'Broad' |
| U | .3 | Arrive Barton Staithe and TURNABOUT | |
| T2 | .3 | Turn sharp right | No sign |
| | .1 | Straight, not right | No sign |
| | .1 | Fork left at Y junction | No sign |
| V | .4 | Straight, not right | No sign |
| W | .2 | Turn right at T junction | Stalham |
| X | .3 | Turn right at T junction | Smallburgh |
| Y | .6 | Turn right, on to A1151 | Stalham |
| Z | .5 | Straight, not left, joining A149, in Low Street | Stalham |
| | | Total mileage on this map: 16.7 | |

# On Route

**Horstead Mill** (See Page 13)

**Horstead**

We liked the cheerfully painted 18th century inn... The Recruiting Sergeant.

**Coltishall**

As it marks the head of navigation on the River Bure, Coltishall is a favourite port of call for boating men and the King's Head and the Rising Sun are both full of Broadland atmosphere. Take time off to look round this village with its pleasant mellow brick Georgian houses, and its interesting church, complete with two round Anglo-Saxon windows, beautiful Norman font, and little 17th century gallery beneath the tower.

**Belaugh**

Attractive village with a small staithe and boatyard, and an interesting church on a high bluff above a great bend in the River Bure.

**Wroxham**

The twin villages of Wroxham and Hoveton are linked together by a hump-backed bridge over the River Bure. The banks of the Bure are alive with boatyards and the water usually crowded with boats, for these twin villages make up the undisputed capital of Broadland... with unrivalled boat hire and provisioning facilities. (See also Page 31.)

**Ashmanhaugh Church**

Has a minute round tower, reputed to be Norfolk's smallest, and stands at the end of a quiet lane. Do not miss the tomb chest of Honor Bacon, who died tragically in 1591, on the eve of her wedding.

**Tunstead Church**

This splendidly ambitious church stands in open country with only two or three houses for company. Light floods in through great plain glass windows, upon the unspoilt interior, and the spirit of medieval times still lingers here. See especially the tall rood screen, with the rood beam above, the gracefully carved sedilia and piscina, and the 14th century south door with its gorgeous wrought iron work.

**Beeston St. Lawrence**

Round towered church with a fascinating Gothick interior inserted in 1803. Do not miss the stylish wall monuments to the Hultons and the Prestons.

**Beeston Hall**

A charming 18th century 'Gothick' mansion, with typical Georgian interiors. The house and its contents reflect the life style over several generations of the Norfolk family who built it, and who still live there... the Prestons. Teas in the Orangery.

**Barton Turf Church**

Its tall square tower rises amongst trees in a pleasant churchyard. See the fine west door, and the vaulted north porch, but above all do not miss the outstandingly beautiful 15th century rood screen, which includes a unique portrait of Henry VI.

**Barton Staithe**

Attractive quiet little staithe at the head of the beautiful Barton Broad, with parking space above the grassy quays.

1. The Recruiting Sergeant, Horstead

2. The Rising Sun, Coltishall

3. Beeston St. Lawrence Church

4. Barton Staithe

| | Miles | Ref | | Directions | Sign-posted |
|---|---|---|---|---|---|
| | .6 | | | Over Wayford Bridge, crossing River Ant | |
| | .9 | A | | Straight, not left, keeping on A149 | Stalham |
| | .4 | B | | Straight, not right | No sign |
| | .1 | | | Bear left, off A149 at entry to Stalham (Keep straight through Stalham) | Stalham |
| | .4 | C | | Over X rds. beyond church (But turn right if you wish to visit Stalham Staithe) | Sutton |
| | .5 | D | | Straight not right, leaving wider road | Hickling |
| | .5 | E | | Turn right at T junction | Catfield |
| | .2 | | | Over small X rds. | Catfield |
| | .3 | | | Sutton church on right | |
| | .1 | F | | Over X rds. (But turn right, then 1st right and 1st left if you wish to visit Sutton Staithe) | Catfield |
| | .4 | G | | Straight, not right | Hickling Broad |
| | .9 | | | Hickling entry signed | |
| | .1 | H | | Over off-set X rds. | Hickling Broad |
| | .3 | | | Hickling Staithe and Pleasure Boat Inn on right | |
| | .4 | I | | Turn right at T junction | 'Marshes' |
| | .2 | J | | Turn left at Y junction | No sign |
| | .4 | K | | Turn left at T junction | No sign |
| | .2 | | | Turn right, on to wider road | No sign |
| | .4 | L | | Straight, not right, twice (But turn right if you wish to visit Hickling church) | No sign |
| | .3 | M | | Fork right | Sea Palling |
| | .3 | | | Remains of Priory visible by farm over to right | |
| | 1.4 | N | | Turn right at T junction, on to B1159 | Waxham |
| | .2 | | | Sea Palling entry signed | |
| | .4 | O | | Bear left by the Hall Inn and... (But go straight if you wish to visit church) | No sign |
| | | | | Bear right (But go left if you wish to visit beach) | Waxham |
| | .8 | P | | Bear left at T junction, off B1159, in Waxham (Walls and gateway on right) | 'Church' |
| | .1 | | | Turn right at T junction (But walk up left if you wish to visit beach) | No sign |
| | .1 | | | Waxham church on right | |
| | .2 | Q | | Turn left, re-joining B1159 | No sign |
| | | | | Total mileage on this map: 11.1 | |

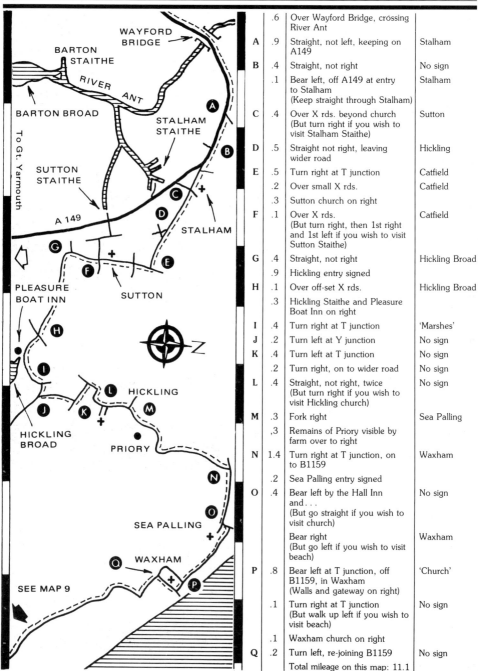

# On Route

## Wayford Bridge

Our road crosses the River Ant about two miles below the limit of navigation for small cruisers. Launches may be hired here for exploration of Barton Broad. There is a path down the northern bank to Huntsett Mill (about a mile).

## Stalham

Bright little market town with cheerful shops, inns and cafes, and many pleasant small Georgian houses. The largely 15th century church contains a magnificent font, with richly carved figures on bowl and stem. There is a lane down to Stalham Staithe which lies beyond the A149. (Turn right at Point C, turn left on to A149, and then turn first right.)

*1. Stalham Staithe*

## Sutton Church

Simple building with a pleasant Jacobean pulpit, some 15th century bench ends, and a real period piece in the shape of a little early 19th century organ. See Route Directions for Sutton Staithe, where there is an excellent hotel.

## Hickling Staithe

This is a classic Broadland port of call, lying at the head of Hickling Broad... with sailing boats, power cruisers, willow trees, boatyards... and above all, the pretty little Pleasure Boat Inn. We remember sitting on its verandah in the autumn sunshine with bread and cheese and a great air of contentment. Hickling Broad and the surrounding marshlands are fine bird watching areas, and those interested should contact the Warden of the Hickling Broad National Nature Reserve. Tel. Hickling 503.

*2. Pleasure Boat Inn, Hickling*

## Hickling Church

Is tucked away from the main road behind an attractive group of houses and cottages. It has a rather severe flint exterior and an over-restored interior, but we liked the tablet in the chancel to John Calthrop (1688) and the urn topped monument in the churchyard to John Byegrave (1818).

## Hickling Hall

A pleasant, mellow brick, early 18th century building, on our left a short distance beyond the church.

*3. In Hickling Churchyard*

## Hickling Priory

The ruins of this 12th and 13th century Augustinian priory are partly visible from our road, in association with a farm.

## Sea Palling

There are fine sands beyond the high dunes, covered here by Marram grass, planted in an endeavour to avoid a recurrence of disastrous floods caused by the sea breaking in. Behind the dunes lies an undistinguished village, although the small church has a lovely old south door and a plain but rather pleasant interior... 14th century font, old benches with poppy heads, neat rood loft stair.

**Waxham** (See Page 19)

*4. Sea Palling Beach*

# Map 9

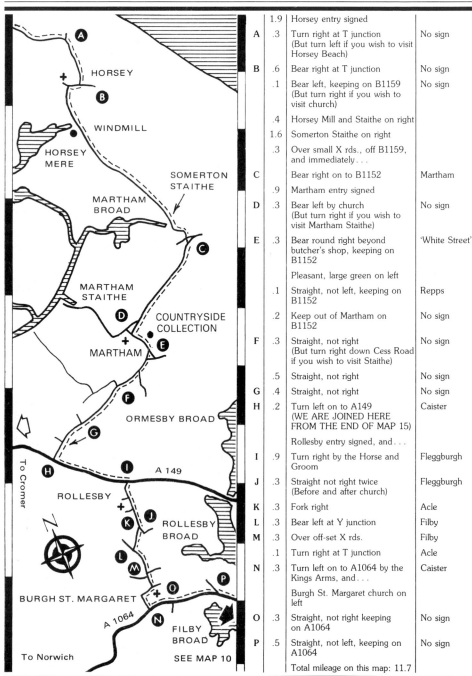

| kms | Ref | Miles | Directions | Signposted |
|---|---|---|---|---|
| | | 1.9 | Horsey entry signed | |
| | A | .3 | Turn right at T junction (But turn left if you wish to visit Horsey Beach) | No sign |
| | B | .6 | Bear right at T junction | No sign |
| | | .1 | Bear left, keeping on B1159 (But turn right if you wish to visit church) | No sign |
| | | .4 | Horsey Mill and Staithe on right | |
| | | 1.6 | Somerton Staithe on right | |
| | | .3 | Over small X rds., off B1159, and immediately... | |
| | C | | Bear right on to B1152 | Martham |
| | | .9 | Martham entry signed | |
| | D | .3 | Bear left by church (But turn right if you wish to visit Martham Staithe) | No sign |
| | E | .3 | Bear round right beyond butcher's shop, keeping on B1152 | 'White Street' |
| | | | Pleasant, large green on left | |
| | | .1 | Straight, not left, keeping on B1152 | Repps |
| | | .2 | Keep out of Martham on B1152 | No sign |
| | F | .3 | Straight, not right (But turn right down Cess Road if you wish to visit Staithe) | No sign |
| | | .5 | Straight, not right | No sign |
| | G | .4 | Straight, not right | No sign |
| | H | .2 | Turn left on to A149 (WE ARE JOINED HERE FROM THE END OF MAP 15) | Caister |
| | | | Rollesby entry signed, and... | |
| | I | .9 | Turn right by the Horse and Groom | Fleggburgh |
| | J | .3 | Straight not right twice (Before and after church) | Fleggburgh |
| | K | .3 | Fork right | Acle |
| | L | .3 | Bear left at Y junction | Filby |
| | M | .3 | Over off-set X rds. | Filby |
| | | .1 | Turn right at T junction | Acle |
| | N | .3 | Turn left on to A1064 by the Kings Arms, and... | Caister |
| | | | Burgh St. Margaret church on left | |
| | O | .3 | Straight, not right keeping on A1064 | No sign |
| | P | .5 | Straight, not left, keeping on A1064 | No sign |
| | | | Total mileage on this map: 11.7 | |

# On Route

### Waxham (See Page 18)

A haunted place with a farm within the walls and gateways of a long vanished mansion...the 15th century Waxham Hall, with a great barn, and a church with a ruined chancel. However the church has a trim porch and a simple interior highlighted by a single dignified Elizabethan tomb with Corinthian columns...Thomas Wodehouse (1571).

### Horsey

Minute village, about a mile from the sea coast, with a small inn, the Nelson Head, and a thatched church with round tower standing in an overgrown churchyard.

### Horsey Mill

Standing at the head of a staithe linked to Horsey Mere, this is a fine drainage windmill in brick, with a wooden capping and well restored sails. It used to pump water into the Mere from the surrounding marshland, and being now owned by the National Trust, is usually open throughout the holiday period. Horsey Mere is noted for its bird life (especially bitterns) and due to its proximity to the sea, is more brackish than most other broads.

### Somerton Staithe

A pleasantly unspoilt spot at the end of a narrow navigable channel up through Martham Broad, with grassy banks, a few houses, and fine views westwards out over the marshes. The sea is about two miles east at Winterton (turn left at Point C).

### Martham

A delightful village with many Georgian houses and cottages, the best of which are grouped around the wide, well kept green. The church has a splendid tower and a fine 15th century font with sculptured figures and an exceptionally well constructed hammerbeam roof (modern). The ambitious Victorian chancel is also unusually pleasing. There are two roads down to two separate staithes on the River Thurne (see Point D and Point F). At both staithes there are boatyards and fine open views across the marshes towards Heigham Sound and Hickling Broad. It is possible to walk down beside the Thurne to Potter Heigham Bridge (see page 25).

### Rollesby

The church lies away from most of the village, with only a pleasant farmhouse and some attractive cottages for company. It stands in an overgrown churchyard and is usually locked. However it has a round tower with octagonal top and inside, two interesting 17th century monuments, especially that to Leonard Mapes (1619), which has 14 kneeling figures.

### Burgh St. Margaret

An undistinguished village with a small church, almost entirely re-built in the 19th century. However it does have two Norman doorways, and inside (usually locked) there is a 16th century brass.

*1. At Horsey Gap*

*2. Horsey Mill*　　*3. Martham Church*

*4. The Green, Martham*

*5. Farm near Rollesby Church*

# Map 10

| kms Ref. Miles | | Directions | Sign-posted |
|---|---|---|---|

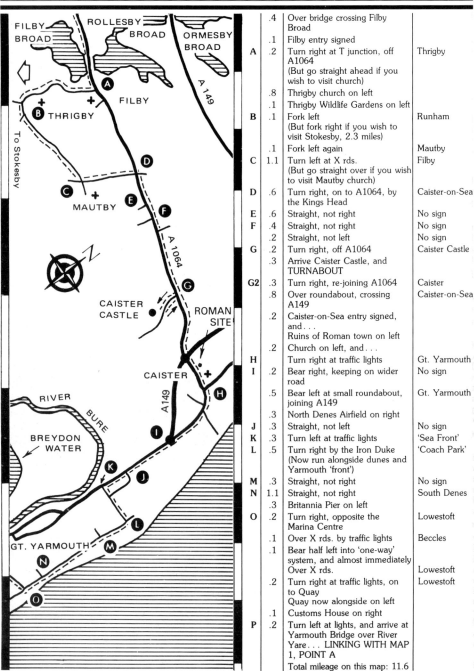

|  | .4 | Over bridge crossing Filby Broad | |
|  | .1 | Filby entry signed | |
| A | .2 | Turn right at T junction, off A1064 (But go straight ahead if you wish to visit church) | Thrigby |
|  | .8 | Thrigby church on left | |
|  | .1 | Thrigby Wildlife Gardens on left | |
| B | .1 | Fork left (But fork right if you wish to visit Stokesby, 2.3 miles) | Runham |
|  | .1 | Fork left again | Mautby |
| C | 1.1 | Turn left at X rds. (But go straight over if you wish to visit Mautby church) | Filby |
| D | .6 | Turn right, on to A1064, by the Kings Head | Caister-on-Sea |
| E | .6 | Straight, not right | No sign |
| F | .4 | Straight, not right | No sign |
|  | .2 | Straight, not left | No sign |
| G | .2 | Turn right, off A1064 | Caister Castle |
|  | .3 | Arrive Caister Castle, and TURNABOUT | |
| G2 | .3 | Turn right, re-joining A1064 | Caister |
|  | .8 | Over roundabout, crossing A149 | Caister-on-Sea |
|  | .2 | Caister-on-Sea entry signed, and . . . Ruins of Roman town on left | |
|  | .2 | Church on left, and . . . | |
| H |  | Turn right at traffic lights | Gt. Yarmouth |
| I | .2 | Bear right, keeping on wider road | No sign |
|  | .5 | Bear left at small roundabout, joining A149 | Gt. Yarmouth |
|  | .3 | North Denes Airfield on right | |
| J | .3 | Straight, not left | No sign |
| K | .3 | Turn left at traffic lights | 'Sea Front' |
| L | .5 | Turn right by the Iron Duke (Now run alongside dunes and Yarmouth 'front') | 'Coach Park' |
| M | .3 | Straight, not right | No sign |
| N | 1.1 | Straight, not right | South Denes |
|  | .3 | Britannia Pier on left | |
| O | .2 | Turn right, opposite the Marina Centre | Lowestoft |
|  | .1 | Over X rds. by traffic lights | Beccles |
|  | .1 | Bear half left into 'one-way' system, and almost immediately Over X rds. | Lowestoft |
|  | .2 | Turn right at traffic lights, on to Quay Quay now alongside on left | Lowestoft |
|  | .1 | Customs House on right | |
| P | .2 | Turn left at lights, and arrive at Yarmouth Bridge over River Yare . . . LINKING WITH MAP 1, POINT A | |
|  |  | Total mileage on this map: 11.6 | |

# On Route

## Filby Broad

Neither Filby Broad, nor Rollesby and Ormesby Broads, to which it is linked, are connected to the navigable system of Broadland waterways, and they are therefore unusually tranquil and provide excellent fishing. It is possible to hire rowing boats from the 'yard' on our left just before Point A.

## Filby

Pleasantly unspoilt village close to the shores of Filby Broad, with a church lying off our route. This has an interesting 14th century north door and a rood screen with figures of eight saints.

1. Filby Broad

## Thrigby Hall Wildlife Gardens

An interesting collection of Asian mammals in pleasantly landscaped grounds, with a gift shop and cafe, and attractions for children.

## Stokesby (A diversion of 2.3 miles)

The cheerful little Ferry Inn at Stokesby is a popular mooring place for boats on passage up the River Bure from Yarmouth. Stokesby itself is a quiet village with a wide green bordered by flowering trees. Do not miss the interesting brasses in the church.

## Mautby

The solitary church contains an octagonal font with an attractive cover and a 14th century sedilia and piscina with intriguing animal heads.

2. The Ferry Inn, Stokesby

## Caister Castle

Ruins of the castle built by Sir John Fastolf (who figures in Shakespeare's Henry VI). Following his death in 1549 the castle fell into the hands of the Paston family, and many of the famous Paston letters were written from here. With its curtain walls, tall tower and moat complete with waterfowl, Caister is a most romantic place. On the far side of a large car park is a modern building housing a well displayed collection of early motor vehicles.

## Caister on Sea

A seaside resort with a fine, wide open beach with a few fishing boats providing a certain amount of character. The much restored church has an ambitious font, and two interesting monuments to members of the Crowe family. The Romans had a harbour town here, and part of its excavated remains are now open to visitors.

3. Caister Castle

## Great Yarmouth continued from Page 3

walls, the Nelson Column (erected in 1817), and St. Nicholas Church, the largest parish church in England. This was bombed in 1942, but has been excellently restored, using woodwork from the 18th century church of St. George (now closed). St. Nicholas's lies at the north east corner of the large market place, in an area with the atmosphere of a miniature cathedral close called Church Plain. Beyond the collection of handsome Georgian houses, are the picturesque 18th century almshouses known as the Fishermen's Hospital.

This is indeed a town full of atmosphere and interest and is well worth exploring.

4. St. Nicholas Church, Great Yarmouth    5. Fishermen's Hospital, Great Yarmouth

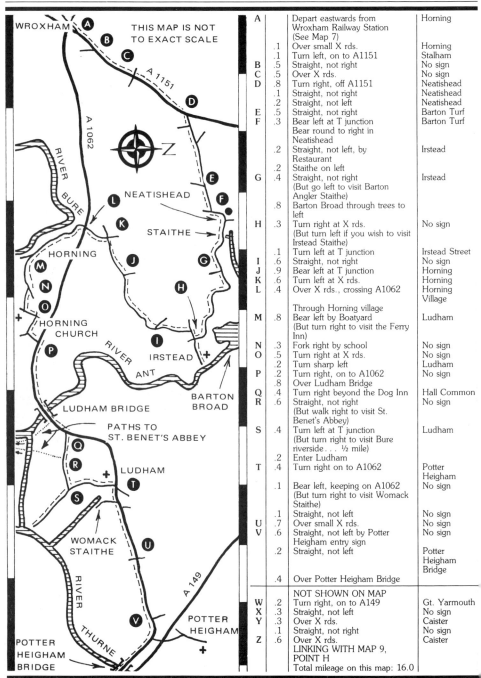

WROXHAM

THIS MAP IS NOT TO EXACT SCALE

A 1151

A 1062

RIVER BURE

NEATISHEAD

STAITHE →

HORNING

RIVER ANT

IRSTEAD

HORNING CHURCH

BARTON BROAD

LUDHAM BRIDGE

PATHS TO ST. BENET'S ABBEY

LUDHAM

WOMACK STAITHE

RIVER THURNE

POTTER HEIGHAM

POTTER HEIGHAM BRIDGE

A 149

| | kms Ref. Miles | Directions | Sign-posted |
|---|---|---|---|
| A | | Depart eastwards from Wroxham Railway Station (See Map 7) | Horning |
| | .1 | Over small X rds. | Horning |
| | .1 | Turn left, on to A1151 | Stalham |
| B | .5 | Straight, not right | No sign |
| C | .5 | Over X rds. | No sign |
| D | .8 | Turn right, off A1151 | Neatishead |
| | .1 | Straight, not right | Neatishead |
| | .2 | Straight, not left | Neatishead |
| E | .5 | Straight, not right | Barton Turf |
| F | .3 | Bear left at T junction | Barton Turf |
| | | Bear round to right in Neatishead | |
| | .2 | Straight, not left, by Restaurant | Irstead |
| | .2 | Staithe on left | |
| G | .4 | Straight, not right (But go left to visit Barton Angler Staithe) | Irstead |
| | .8 | Barton Broad through trees to left | |
| H | .3 | Turn right at X rds. (But turn left if you wish to visit Irstead Staithe) | No sign |
| | .1 | Turn left at T junction | Irstead Street |
| I | .6 | Straight, not right | No sign |
| J | .9 | Bear left at T junction | Horning |
| K | .6 | Turn left at X rds. | Horning |
| L | .4 | Over X rds., crossing A1062 | Horning Village |
| | | Through Horning village | |
| M | .8 | Bear left by Boatyard (But turn right to visit the Ferry Inn) | Ludham |
| N | .3 | Fork right by school | No sign |
| O | .5 | Turn right at X rds. | No sign |
| | .2 | Turn sharp left | Ludham |
| P | .2 | Turn right, on to A1062 | No sign |
| | .8 | Over Ludham Bridge | |
| Q | .4 | Turn right beyond the Dog Inn | Hall Common |
| R | .6 | Straight, not right (But walk right to visit St. Benet's Abbey) | No sign |
| S | .4 | Turn left at T junction (But turn right to visit Bure riverside . . . ½ mile) | Ludham |
| | .2 | Enter Ludham | |
| T | .4 | Turn right on to A1062 | Potter Heigham |
| | .1 | Bear left, keeping on A1062 (But turn right to visit Womack Staithe) | No sign |
| | .1 | Straight, not left | No sign |
| U | .7 | Over small X rds. | No sign |
| V | .6 | Straight, not left by Potter Heigham entry sign | No sign |
| | .2 | Straight, not left | Potter Heigham Bridge |
| | .4 | Over Potter Heigham Bridge | |
| | | NOT SHOWN ON MAP | |
| W | .2 | Turn right, on to A149 | Gt. Yarmouth |
| X | .3 | Straight, not left | No sign |
| Y | .3 | Over X rds. | Caister |
| | .3 | Straight, not right | No sign |
| Z | .6 | Over X rds. | Caister |
| | | LINKING WITH MAP 9, POINT H | |
| | | Total mileage on this map: 16.0 | |

# On Route

## Neatishead
Attractive little village with mellow brick Georgian houses, at the head of a wooded creek running westwards from Barton Broad.

## Barton Broad
Lovely tree bordered broad on the River Ant, tantalising glimpses of which can be seen to the left of our route between Neatishead and Irstead.

## Irstead
A quiet woody place with a round towered church close to a small staithe, which lies on the Ant, just south of Barton Broad. The church contains several items of interest including a 14th century font with carved figures, a screen with painted saints, poppy head bench ends, some with animal carvings, and an iron-work cross on the south door (probably by the craftsman who made the knocker at Tunstead . . . See Page 15).

## Horning
One of the best loved Broadland boating centres, with one long street bordering the north bank of the Bure. All is neat and trim, with mellow brick and reed thatch . . . with boatyards and inns, cottages and shops. There used to be a ferry across towards Woodbastwick (see page 31), but this together with the Ferry Boat Inn was bombed during the War. The inn was re-built, but the car ferry service was never restored. Horning church lies well away from the village, and has a tall octagonal font and a few interesting bench ends (see especially . . . the devil pushing a man into a dragon's mouth).

## Ludham Bridge
Popular mooring point on the River Ant, complete with boatyard, stores and an inn (The Dog) a short distance away.

## St. Benet's Abbey
Reached on foot from either Ludham Bridge (1.75 miles) or on foot from Point R (1 mile), these ruins of a vast Benedictine abbey, founded before the Conquest, are made doubly fascinating by the presence in their midst of the massive cone of a ruined windmill.

## Ludham
Pleasant village with several interesting old houses and a fine large church. See especially the ancient parish alms box, the beautifully sculptured font, the attractive screen, the painting of the Crucifixion and the splendid hammer-beam roof.

## Womack Staithe
Delightful moorings at the head of Womack Water, a narrow waterway which branches off the River Thurne about a mile away.

## Potter Heigham
The old village lies some distance from the bridge (see page 25) and has been left undisturbed by boating men. It has a 14th century church with an earlier round tower and thatched roof

## Potter Heigham Bridge (See Page 25)

1. Neatishead Staithe

2. Barton Road

3. Below Ludham Bridge

4. At Horning Ferry

5. Potter Heigham Bridge

23

# Map 12

| Miles | | | | Directions | Sign-posted |
|---|---|---|---|---|---|
| | kms Ref. Miles | | | | |
| A | | | | Depart northwards from Beccles Service Station, Beccles, into town centre (LEAVING FROM MAP 3, POINT Q) | Great Yarmouth |
| B | .3 | | | Bear right, immediately beyond Kings Head | Norwich |
| | .1 | | | Church on left (Follow out of Beccles on main road) | |
| C | .4 | | | Bear left and over bridge crossing Waveney | Norwich |
| D | .8 | | | Straight, not left, beyond Swan Inn, Gillingham (WATCH NEXT JUNCTIONS WITH CARE... NEW ROAD BEING BUILT WHEN OUR ROUTE LAST REVISED) | Bungay |
| | .2 | | | Bear left on to A146 | Norwich |
| E | .2 | | | Bear right at large roundabout, on to A143 (Watch carefully for access to the three Gillingham churches) | Great Yarmouth |
| | .1 | | | Straight, not left, keeping on A143 | Great Yarmouth |
| F | .5 | | | Straight, not left, keeping on A143 | No sign |
| G | .5 | | | Fork right, off A143 | Aldeby |
| H | .5 | | | Straight, not left | Aldeby |
| I | 1.0 | | | Straight, not left | No sign |
| | .2 | | | Bear right in Aldeby | Aldeby Street |
| | .1 | | | Church on left | |
| J | .4 | | | Straight, not left | No sign |
| K | .6 | | | Straight, not left by cottages Pleasant open road with views over Waveney Valley. Large gravel pits to left. Beware of steep drops near edge of road | No sign |
| L | .5 | | | Bear round to left | No sign |
| M | .2 | | | Turn sharp right at T junction | No sign |
| N | .7 | | | Bear right at T junction, and almost immediately... Fork left | Burgh Staithe / No sign |
| O | .9 | | | Turn left at small X rds. (But turn right to visit Burgh St Peter Staithe) (Or go straight over to visit church) | Haddiscoe |
| P | .3 | | | Straight, not left by barns | No sign |
| Q | 1.2 | | | Turn left at T junction | Burgh St. Peter |
| R | .4 | | | Turn right at T junction | 'Church Lane' |
| S | .5 | | | Turn right at T junction, and... Wheatacre church on right | Haddiscoe |
| T | .2 | | | Turn right, keeping on wider road | Haddiscoe |
| | | | | Total mileage on this map: 10.8 | |

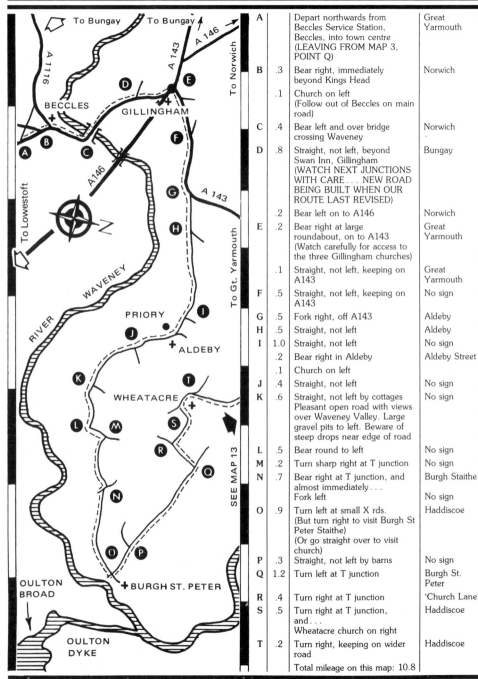

24

# On Route

## Potter Heigham Bridge (See Page 22)

Medieval stone bridge, low enough to make it necessary for some boats to wait for low tide. There are inns, hotels, shops, boatyards and every facility for the holidaymaker.

## Beccles (See also Page 6)

Busy market town with a wealth of attractive houses and shops, with the 18th century providing most of the best specimens. The church has a fine ninety-two feet high detached tower (splendid views), and an equally fine vaulted porch. The interior is on a very grand scale, but it appears to contain few items of real interest to visitors. The churchyard overlooks steep slopes down to the curving River Waveney, and boats can just be seen through the trees. However the best riverside views can be obtained from the bridge at the far end of picturesque Northgate Street (beyond Point C).

## Gillingham

An unexceptional village on the edge of the Waveney marshlands. Beyond the village there are three churches within a stone's throw of each other . . . the creeper covered ruins of a medieval tower, the largely neo-Norman parish church (St. Mary's) and a red brick Italian style Roman Catholic church. There are pleasant glimpses of 17th and 18th century Gillingham Hall from St. Mary's churchyard.

## Aldeby

The village has no special features, but we liked its quiet setting overlooking the Waveney valley marsh country. A farm near the church incorporates the remains of a small 12th century priory, but this is not apparent from the road. The church is Norman in origin and has an attractive Norman west doorway. Its long narrow interior has been much restored, but will certainly interest those in search of the architecturally unusual.

## Burgh St. Peter

Our route misses the village but Burgh St. Peter church is most attractively sited looking out across the Waveney valley towards Oulton Broad. The unique toy building brick' tower is believed to date from the 16th century, although the narrow thatched nave and chancel are much earlier. See especially the font with heads round the bowl and the pulpit with copper plates commemorating numerous members of the Boycott family, who were rectors here for no less than 135 years. The once quiet staithe below the church is now a fully developed marina, known as the Waveney River Centre. There is an hotel and shop, and fine views out across the Waveney to the Oulton Marshes.

## Wheatacre

A scattered, undramatic village in the centre of the tongue of high ground bordered on three sides by the Waveney marshes. Wheatacre church has a handsome tower of chequered brick and flint. Its octagonal font has lions and shields with traces of medieval painting. Church usually locked.

1. Quiet Moorings at Beccles

2. Cottage opposite the church, Aldeby

3. Burch St. Peter Church

4. At the Waveney River Centre, Burgh St. Peter

Miles

# Map 13

kms
Ref.
Miles

Directions

Sign-posted

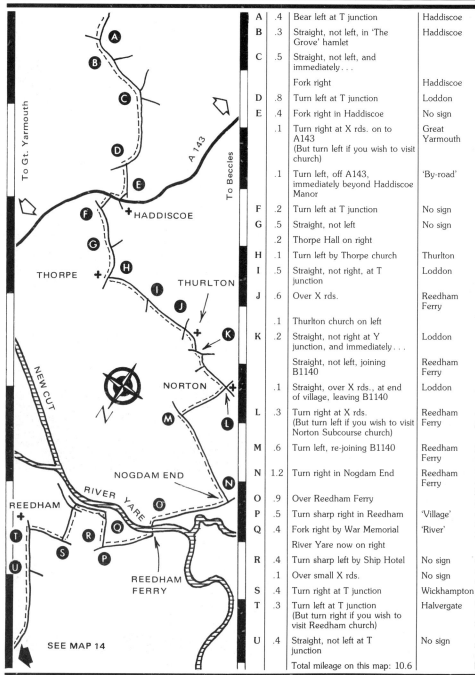

| | Ref. | Miles | Directions | Sign-posted |
|---|---|---|---|---|
| A | .4 | | Bear left at T junction | Haddiscoe |
| B | .3 | | Straight, not left, in 'The Grove' hamlet | Haddiscoe |
| C | .5 | | Straight, not left, and immediately... | |
| | | | Fork right | Haddiscoe |
| D | .8 | | Turn left at T junction | Loddon |
| E | .4 | | Fork right in Haddiscoe | No sign |
| | .1 | | Turn right at X rds. on to A143 (But turn left if you wish to visit church) | Great Yarmouth |
| | .1 | | Turn left, off A143, immediately beyond Haddiscoe Manor | 'By-road' |
| F | .2 | | Turn left at T junction | No sign |
| G | .5 | | Straight, not left | No sign |
| | .2 | | Thorpe Hall on right | |
| H | .1 | | Turn left by Thorpe church | Thurlton |
| I | .5 | | Straight, not right, at T junction | Loddon |
| J | .6 | | Over X rds. | Reedham Ferry |
| | .1 | | Thurlton church on left | |
| K | .2 | | Straight, not right at Y junction, and immediately... | Loddon |
| | | | Straight, not left, joining B1140 | Reedham Ferry |
| | .1 | | Straight, over X rds., at end of village, leaving B1140 | Loddon |
| L | .3 | | Turn right at X rds. (But turn left if you wish to visit Norton Subcourse church) | Reedham Ferry |
| M | .6 | | Turn left, re-joining B1140 | Reedham Ferry |
| N | 1.2 | | Turn right in Nogdam End | Reedham Ferry |
| O | .9 | | Over Reedham Ferry | |
| P | .5 | | Turn sharp right in Reedham | 'Village' |
| Q | .4 | | Fork right by War Memorial | 'River' |
| | | | River Yare now on right | |
| R | .4 | | Turn sharp left by Ship Hotel | No sign |
| | .1 | | Over small X rds. | No sign |
| S | .4 | | Turn right at T junction | Wickhampton |
| T | .3 | | Turn left at T junction (But turn right if you wish to visit Reedham church) | Halvergate |
| U | .4 | | Straight, not left at T junction | No sign |
| | | | Total mileage on this map: 10.6 | |

# On Route

## Haddiscoe

Has a fascinating church, beautifully sited on a small hill, with an Anglo-Saxon round tower and many Norman features. There is a lovely Norman south doorway, with a figure of the same period over it, and a medieval door ornamented with splendid ironwork.

## Thorpe-next-Haddiscoe

We particularly liked the attractive 17th century Thorpe Hall, looking out over the fields beside our road. In our view it typifies the vernacular building style of East Anglia . . . with its unpretentious charm and quiet dignity. Just beyond it lies the small church, set in a spotless, well mown churchyard. The lower part of its round tower is unmistakably Anglo-Saxon (note windows and blank arcading).

## Thurlton

Like many of the villages through which we have passed Thurlton has little to show apart from its church. This has a square tower and thatched roof. It has a Norman south doorway, small but well preserved. The north doorway has attractively elongated angels in the spandrels, and a pleasant old traceried door. We also liked the medieval wall painting of St. Christopher and the Margaret Denny monument (1717) with its heraldry and winged cherub.

## Norton Subcourse

An undistinguished village, but the church is larger than most we have seen recently. It has a round tower and a broad interior, well lit by the wide 14th century traceried window, with its great expanse of clear glass. The pink and white colour wash provides an 18th century flavour, and this feeling is enhanced by the classical pilasters supporting a tie beam. See also the Purbeck marble font and the very pretty group of sedilia and piscina.

## Reedham Ferry

This is a wide, open marshland place, where the River Yare is crossed by a small car ferry, the last descendant of the old Norfolk horse ferries, (although this craft is diesel operated). On the north bank, in the shade of luxuriant willows, lies the cheerful Ferry Inn. Boats pass to and fro, and the clank of the ferry chain provides an almost constant background to the cries of birds and the bleat of sheep out on the great marshlands.

## Reedham

The busy quay at Reedham is another favourite of ours, with its attractively painted inn sign, its trees overhanging the water, the broad views southwards out over Norton Marshes, and, of course, the coming and going of boats of all shapes and sizes . . . a particularly good place for motorists to savour the atmosphere of Broadland. Reedham church lies away to the north-east of the village. It has a thatched roof and a tall, handsome tower. See especially the pretty font and the fine tomb chest to Henry Berney, complete with husband, wife, five sons and four daughters.

1. Haddiscoe Church

2. Norman Sculpture, Haddiscoe

3. Thorpe Church

4. At Reedham Ferry

5. Reedham Staithe

27

Miles

# Map 14

kms
Ref.
Miles

Directions

Sign-
posted

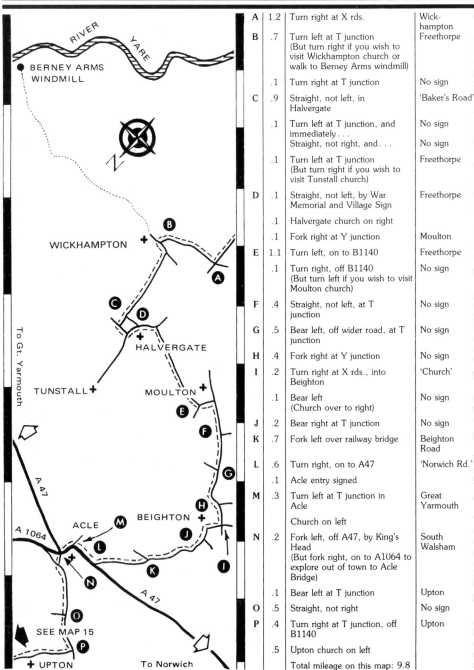

| | kms Ref. Miles | Directions | Sign-posted |
|---|---|---|---|
| A | 1.2 | Turn right at X rds. | Wickhampton |
| B | .7 | Turn left at T junction (But turn right if you wish to visit Wickhampton church or walk to Berney Arms windmill) | Freethorpe |
| | .1 | Turn right at T junction | No sign |
| C | .9 | Straight, not left, in Halvergate | 'Baker's Road' |
| | .1 | Turn left at T junction, and immediately . . . Straight, not right, and . . . | No sign No sign |
| | .1 | Turn left at T junction (But turn right if you wish to visit Tunstall church) | Freethorpe |
| D | .1 | Straight, not left, by War Memorial and Village Sign | Freethorpe |
| | .1 | Halvergate church on right | |
| | .1 | Fork right at Y junction | Moulton |
| E | 1.1 | Turn left, on to B1140 | Freethorpe |
| | .1 | Turn right, off B1140 (But turn left if you wish to visit Moulton church) | No sign |
| F | .4 | Straight, not left, at T junction | No sign |
| G | .5 | Bear left, off wider road, at T junction | No sign |
| H | .4 | Fork right at Y junction | No sign |
| I | .2 | Turn right at X rds., into Beighton | 'Church' |
| | .1 | Bear left (Church over to right) | No sign |
| J | .2 | Bear right at T junction | No sign |
| K | .7 | Fork left over railway bridge | Beighton Road |
| L | .6 | Turn right, on to A47 | 'Norwich Rd.' |
| | .1 | Acle entry signed | |
| M | .3 | Turn left at T junction in Acle | Great Yarmouth |
| | | Church on left | |
| N | .2 | Fork left, off A47, by King's Head (But fork right, on to A1064 to explore out of town to Acle Bridge) | South Walsham |
| | .1 | Bear left at T junction | Upton |
| O | .5 | Straight, not right | No sign |
| P | .4 | Turn right at T junction, off B1140 | Upton |
| | .5 | Upton church on left | |
| | | Total mileage on this map: 9.8 | |

# On Route

### Wickhampton Church

Stands on the edge of the marshes together with a few farms and cottages. Obtain the key from Thatch Farm (on our right just before church), as the interior is well worth the trouble. See especially the wall paintings including St. Christoper (inevitably), dancing skeletons (The Three Quick and The Three Dead), and a particularly attractive series of "The Seven Acts of Mercy". See also the two tomb recesses containing the 13th century effigies of a knight and a lady.

### Berney Arms Windmill

It is possible to walk from Wickhampton across the marshes to this seventy feet high windmill (the highest in Norfolk or Suffolk) on the banks of the Yare. This is about three miles, and should not be attempted after heavy rain.

### Tunstall

Remote hamlet with a small ruined church. A tablet indicates that the chancel was blocked up in 1705 and the ivy looks as if it has been growing ever since . . . all rather sad.

### Halvergate

Pleasant village with thatched houses and many trees, centred upon a little triangular green . . . all in surprising contrast to the great expanse of Halvergate Marshes to the immediate east, with its windmills and long dykes. The church has a fine south doorway and an interesting palimpsest brass (re-used by turning over and engraving on the reverse), with the head of a Franciscan friar on the earlier side.

### Moulton

Charmingly sited church, backed by trees and approached over a field road. It has a small conical topped tower, and some pleasant Jacobean woodwork within.

### Beighton

The church here is usually locked, but it contains a fascinating 17th century chest with poker-worked decoration illustrating the story of Susanna and the Elders.

### Acle

Busy little town astride the main Norwich–Yarmouth road, with Acle Bridge (a mile to the north-east) a popular port of call for boating men. The church has a small round tower with an octagonal top and there are attractive pollarded limes in the churchyard. Inside there is a fine rood screen, a delightful little miniature medieval font, and a handsome 18th century monument.

### Upton

A fine church looking out over quiet countryside with a flying dragon weather vane atop its recently re-built tower. In the churchyard there is a tombstone with a Norfolk wherry carved on it, and inside a gorgeous, richly sculptured 14th century font, and a rood screen with eight painted figures.

1. Moulton Church

2. Wickhampton Tower    3. Tomb at Wickhampton

4. Berney Arms Mill

5. The Bridge Inn, Acle

29

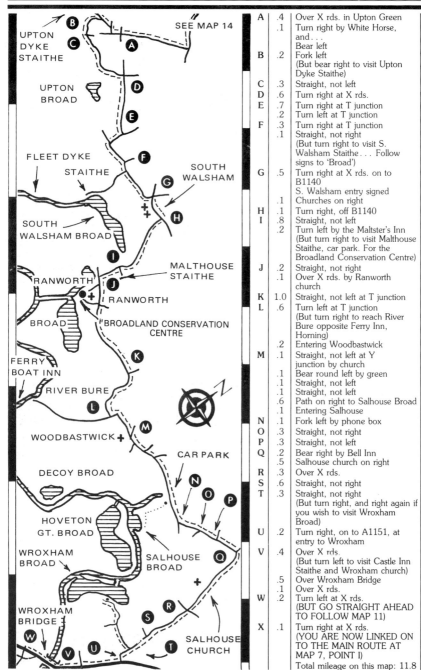

| Ref | Miles | Directions | Signposted |
|---|---|---|---|
| A | .4 | Over X rds. in Upton Green | 'Marshes' |
|   | .1 | Turn right by White Horse, and . . . | 'Dyke' |
|   |   | Bear left | 'Dyke' |
| B | .2 | Fork left | No sign |
|   |   | (But bear right to visit Upton Dyke Staithe) | |
| C | .3 | Straight, not left | No sign |
| D | .6 | Turn right at X rds. | S. Walsham |
| E | .7 | Turn right at T junction | S. Walsham |
|   | .2 | Turn left at T junction | S. Walsham |
| F | .3 | Turn right at T junction | S. Walsham |
|   | .1 | Straight, not right | S. Walsham |
|   |   | (But turn right to visit S. Walsham Staithe . . . Follow signs to 'Broad') | |
| G | .5 | Turn right at X rds. on to B1140 | Panxworth |
|   | .1 | S. Walsham entry signed Churches on right | |
| H | .1 | Turn right, off B1140 | Ranworth |
| I | .8 | Straight, not left | No sign |
|   | .2 | Turn left by the Maltster's Inn | Panxworth |
|   |   | (But turn right to visit Malthouse Staithe, car park. For the Broadland Conservation Centre) | |
| J | .2 | Straight, not right | No sign |
|   | .1 | Over X rds. by Ranworth church | Woodbastwick |
| K | 1.0 | Straight, not left at T junction | Woodbastwick |
| L | .6 | Turn left at T junction | Salhouse |
|   |   | (But turn right to reach River Bure opposite Ferry Inn, Horning) | |
|   | .2 | Entering Woodbastwick | |
| M | .1 | Straight, not left at Y junction by church | Salhouse |
|   | .1 | Bear round left by green | No sign |
|   | .1 | Straight, not left | Salhouse |
|   | .1 | Straight, not left | No sign |
|   | .6 | Path on right to Salhouse Broad | |
|   | .1 | Entering Salhouse | |
| N | .1 | Fork left by phone box | Plumstead |
| O | .3 | Straight, not right | Rackheath |
| P | .3 | Straight, not left | No sign |
| Q | .2 | Bear right by Bell Inn | Wroxham |
|   | .5 | Salhouse church on right | |
| R | .3 | Over X rds. | Wroxham |
| S | .6 | Straight, not right | No sign |
| T | .3 | Straight, not right | Wroxham |
|   |   | (But turn right, and right again if you wish to visit Wroxham Broad) | |
| U | .2 | Turn right, on to A1151, at entry to Wroxham | Stalham |
| V | .4 | Over X rds. | Wroxham |
|   |   | (But turn left to visit Castle Inn Staithe and Wroxham church) | |
|   | .5 | Over Wroxham Bridge | |
|   | .1 | Over X rds. | No sign |
| W | .2 | Turn left at X rds. | Coltishall |
|   |   | (BUT GO STRAIGHT AHEAD TO FOLLOW MAP 11) | |
| X | .1 | Turn right at X rds. | Tunstead |
|   |   | (YOU ARE NOW LINKED ON TO THE MAIN ROUTE AT MAP 7, POINT I) | |
|   |   | Total mileage on this map: 11.8 | |

# On Route

## Upton Dyke Staithe
We came here one late October afternoon and were enchanted with the quietness of the place, with its handful of boats and its wide misty views.

## Upton Broad
Enquire at Cargate Green (Point D) for details of fishing boat hire on this small quiet broad.

## South Walsham Staithe
This staithe is attractively situated, looking out across the tree bordered waters of South Walsham Outer Broad.

## South Walsham
The large, well mown churchyard shelters not one, but two churches . . . St. Laurence, which is derelict, and St. Mary's, a 14th century building with several interesting features.

## Malthouse Staithe, Ranworth
Popular port of call at the southern end of lovely Ranworth Broad, complete with buffet and shop in the old malthouses. Park here to visit the Broadland Conservation Centre, which is approached via a 400 yard Nature Trail. The centre has a gallery with observation windows looking out over the Broad, and there are fascinating displays illustrating many aspects of the Broadland habitat.

## Ranworth
One of the finest Broadland views is obtained from the roof of Ranworth's tall tower, (open week-days only) looking out over Malthouse Broad, and across the wide Bure valley to St. Benet's Abbey, and on a clear day, south-westwards to Norwich spire. The interior of Ranworth church is a treasure-house of beautiful things. The rood screen, with its glorious medieval paintings is probably the finest in the country, but see also the medieval lectern, the pulpit with its linen-fold panelling, and the stalls with their misericords and poppy heads.

## Woodbastwick
Beautifully maintained 'estate village' complete with village green, thatched cottages, well-house and village sign. The church was restored by Sir Giles Gilbert Scott and is still wonderfully cared for, like the rest of the village.

## Salhouse Broad
There is a car park on the right immediately before the entry to Salhouse, and a path (½ mile) leads from it to this, one of the loveliest broads accessible to the walker. It is an enchanted spot, with heron and wildfowl usually to be seen amongst the surrounding trees.

## Wroxham Broad
Turn right at Point T, and turn right again.)
There is a public car park enclosure on the wooded shores of Wroxham Broad, an excellent place from which to watch boating activity on this the 'Queen of the Broads'.

## Castle Inn Staithe, Wroxham
A quiet riverside place, not far from Wroxham church.

1. Upton Dyke Staithe    2. Ransworth Screen — detail

3. View from Ranworth Tower

4. Woodbastwick Green

5. Salhouse Broad    Photograph by Jarrold & Sons Ltd.

# INDEX